COULD A CROCODILE PLAY BASKETBALL?

...and other questions

Aleksei Bitskoff &
Camilla de la Bédoyère

QED

Saltwater crocodiles are the **largest** crocodiles in

They live in rivers by the jungle, and in the sea.

Design: Duck Egg Blue
Editor: Carly Madden
Editorial Director: Victoria Garrard
Art Director: Laura Roberts-Jensen
Associate Publisher: Maxime Boucknooghe
Publisher: Zeta Jones

First published in the UK in 2015 by
QED Publishing
Part of The Quarto Group
The Old Brewery
6 Blundell Street
London N7 9BH

www.qed-publishing.co.uk

A catalogue record for this book is available from the British Library.

ISBN 978 1 78171 586 4

Printed in China

the world. They have HUGE jaws and lots of teeth.

Imagine if a crocodile came to stay.
What would he do?

What if a crocodile went to the funfair?

He would have fun riding on a **SPOOKY** ghost train, but he wouldn't be very **frightened.**

There are few animals in the jungle that are brave enough to fight a crocodile...

...he's too big and scary!

Would a crocodile enjoy a snowball fight?

No! He would be a cross croc.

Crocodiles are reptiles, and reptiles cannot move when they are very cold.

Chilly crocs have to snooze until the sun comes out and warms them up.

But a cold croc might make a good...

...snow-croc!

Could a crocodile play basketball?

Yes, he could shoot a ball
through
the
hoop,
no problem!

The biggest crocodiles are
6 metres long.

They can run, stand on their back feet and even leap into the air!

Crocodiles can run faster than most people.

What if a crocodile was very hungry?

He might begin his meal with a mouthful of stones!

Crocodiles swallow stones to help **grind up** the food in their stomachs.

Then he would tuck into a **giant plate** of food.

He could eat 500 kg in one go. That's about

5,000

ham sandwiches!

Would a crocodile like to play with teddies?

He might have **huge**, powerful jaws, but a crocodile could be gentle with teddies.

Crocodiles don't have pushchairs
for their babies, so in the jungle
they carry their babies down to
the river in their...

...enormous mouths!

Some crocodile dads
watch over their babies
to keep them safe.

What if a crocodile visited a castle?

He could swim in the moat.

Or he might pretend to be a knight...

His skin is almost as strong as a suit of armour because it is **covered in scales**.

The large scales on a crocodile's back have plates of bone inside them. Even another crocodile has trouble biting through them!

What would a crocodile like to do for fun?

He would enjoy a game of crazy golf, but he wouldn't need a golf club. He could...

...WHACK the ball...

...with his **mighty tail** instead.

Crocodiles need strong tails because they use them for swimming in rivers, especially when they are chasing fish.

They also use their tail as a handy weapon!

What would a crocodile do if he lost a tooth?

He could leave one of his **BIG, shiny teeth** for the tooth fairy!

actual size!

Crocodiles have about 66 teeth, but if one tooth falls out a new one **grows** to replace it!

A crocodile grows about **3,000 teeth** in its lifetime – that's about **60** times more teeth than you will ever have.

That's a lot of money from the tooth fairy!

Would a crocodile enjoy a sleepover?

Crocodiles don't like to sleep in beds.
They prefer to sleep in water.

He would have to find a watery place that's big enough
for him to **stretch out**.

Everyone would need to **tiptoe** around him, as crocodiles have incredible hearing – even underwater.

It's not a good idea to disturb a
sleeping crocodile!

More about saltwater crocodiles

Crocodile is pointing to the places where he lives.
Can you see where you live?

FACT FILE

There are 13 types of crocodile and two types of alligator.

There were crocodile-like animals living alongside the dinosaurs, millions of years ago.

Saltwater crocodiles lay up to 90 eggs in a huge nest near the riverbank.

Male crocodiles can grow twice as big as females.

Crocodiles can live a long time. They may live to be as old as 100!

Saltwater crocodiles are the largest reptiles in the world.

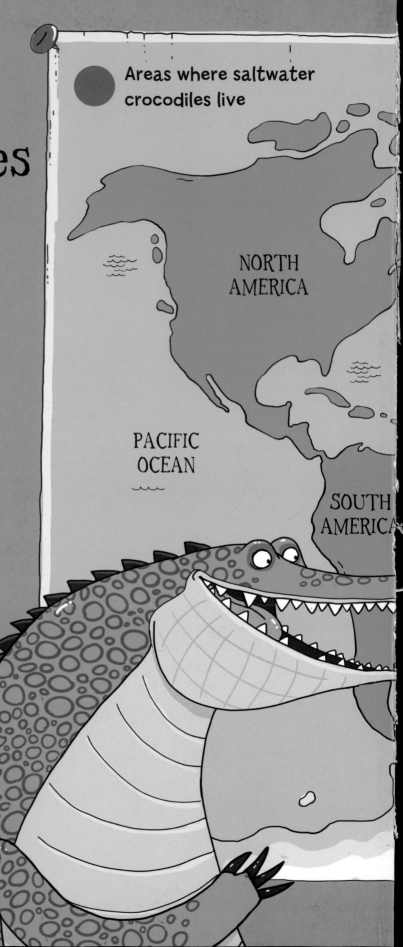

Areas where saltwater crocodiles live

NORTH AMERICA

PACIFIC OCEAN

SOUTH AMERICA

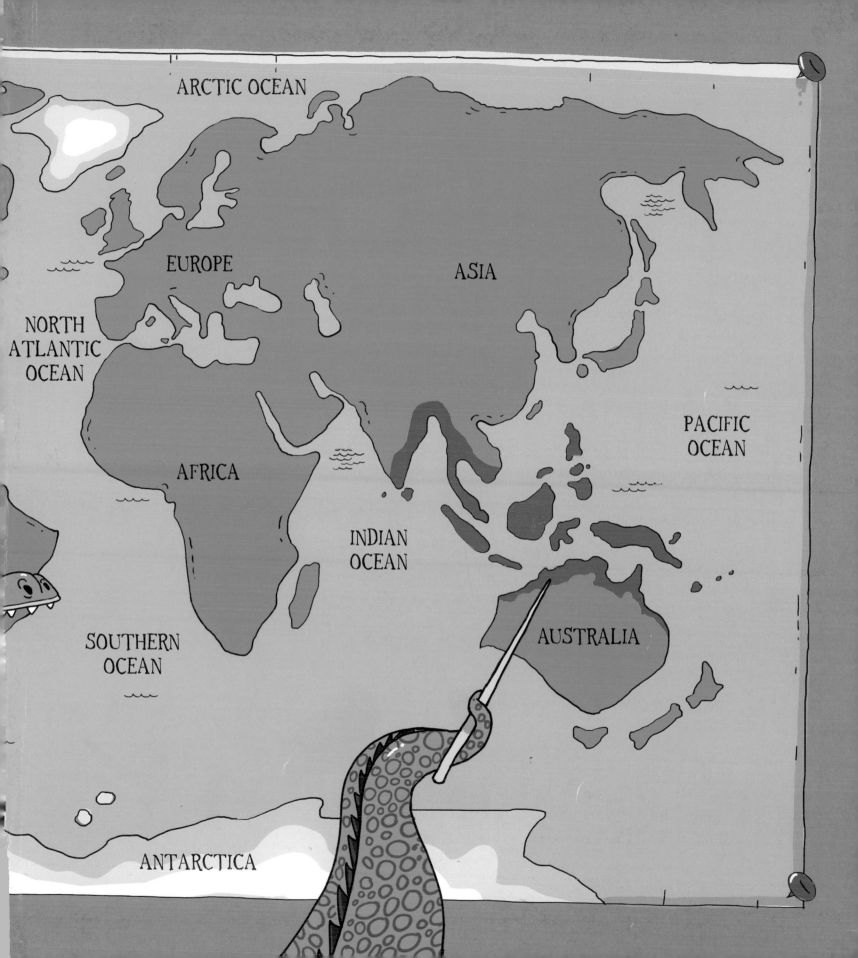

Greetings from Australia!

POST CARD

I'm on my way home now and can't wait to dive into the lovely lagoon and go fishing. Thank you for looking after me!

I had lots of fun at the fair but my favourite holiday treat was crazy golf. I can't wait to teach my crocodile friends how to play!

Love,
Crocodile ✗

SENT BY SALTWATER CROCODILE POST
NORTHERN TERRITORY, AUSTRALIA

1ST

Mr and Mrs Snap
118 Spikey Lane
Poole
DH6 4WP
UK

1704092201122528877